Key Stage 2 English Spelling & Vocabulary

WORKBOOK 4

Intermediate Level

Dr Stephen C Curran

with Warren Vokes

Edited by Mark Schofield

This book belongs to

ae
PUBLICATIONS

Accelerated Education Publications Ltd

team	steam	scream
gleam	slave	shave
grave	cape	front
month	Monday	ton

Exercise 70a

1) The weekend had been fine but on __Monday__ the weather changed.

2) He traced around his hand and then cut out the __front__ .

3) The children enjoyed __playing__ games at William's birthday party.

4) The jewel began to __gleam__ when she held it up to the light.

5) The school's netball __team__ beat their main rivals in the final match.

6) We meet twelve times a year on the first Tuesday of each __month__ .

7) It was raining heavily so he put on his __cape__ which he kept in his saddlebag.

8) Sophie was __staying__ with her grandmother while her mother was in hospital.

9) "I __wonder__ if he'll remember it's my birthday," she thought.

10) He heard his wife __scream__ and ran to help her.

Score ◻ 10

Exercise 70b

11) The water in the kettle was boiling and the __steam__ pressure was lifting the lid.

12) "Michael, come here to the __ton__ of the class and read out your poem."

13) As a special __treat__ her parents took her to the theme park.

14) "I was just __saying__ to my friend that I haven't seen you for many years."

15) It was a very __grave__ situation with serious consequences.

16) The carpenter used a plane to __shave__ off a very small amount of wood.

17) The imperial weight of one __slave__ is equal to 2,240 pounds or 1,016 kilograms.

18) The crew finished ten seconds ahead of the others and __won__ the race easily.

19) William Wilberforce led the campaign to end the __shape__ trade.

20) Instead of __paying__ with her credit card she paid with cash.

Score ◻ 10

2

Across

70

2. About 4 weeks or 30 days.
6. To remove hair with a razor.
7. Giving money for something.
8. A person forced to work for another.
10. First day of the working week.
11. Group forming a side in a sports competition.
13. Amazed admiration or awe.
14. Entertainment paid for by somebody else.
15. Burial place of a dead body.
16. Past participle of '*win*'.

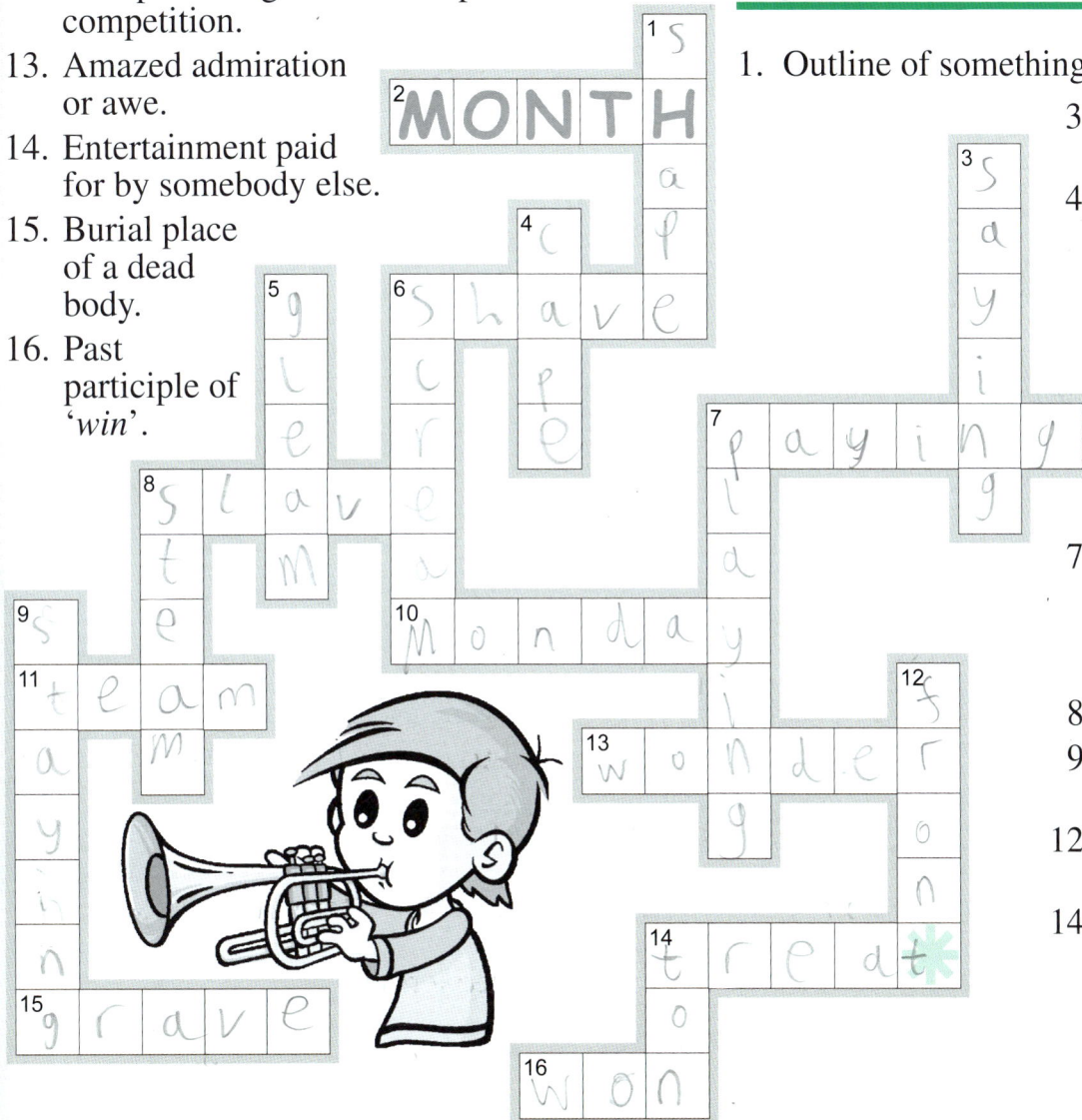

Put the mystery letter (✳) into the box marked **70** below. Add in the mystery letters from puzzles **71** to **77** then rearrange them to make **Oliver's Mystery Word**. The clue is **MUSICAL INSTRUMENT**.

Down

1. Outline of something's form.
3. A proverbial expression.
4. A sleeveless outer garment that hangs loosely from the shoulders.
5. To shine brightly and continuously.
6. Loud, piercing, high-pitched cry.
7. Engaging in enjoyable activity for the sake of amusement.
8. Vaporised water.
9. Remaining in the same place.
12. A part or surface that faces forward.
14. Imperial unit of weight.

Crossword filled answers:

2 Across: MONTH
6 Across: SHAVE
7 Across: PAYING
8 Across: SLAVE
10 Across: MONDAY
11 Across: TEAM
13 Across: WONDER
14 Across: TREAT
15 Across: GRAVE
16 Across: WON

Down:
3: SAYING
5: GLEE
6: SCREAM
7: PLAYING
8: STEAM
9: STAYING
11: TAYIN
12: FRONT

	70	71	72	73	74	75	76	77
Enter your mystery letters here:	t	c	e	n	i			

Now rearrange them:

Mystery Word: t c e ...

Score
/20

Across

71

2. A funny story.
4. Ringing of bells.
6. Dramatic compositions or productions.
9. Volunteer to do something.
11. Excessively proud.
12. Get.
15. Loud noise following lightning.
17. Metal rod for stirring a fire.
18. Near in space or time.
19. Past tense of *'strike'*.

Down

1. Past tense of *'ride'*.
3. To flap the wings rapidly.
4. Speak to God or other being.
5. Simple and ordinary in nature or appearance.
7. Happening quickly and unexpectedly.
8. Map of the Earth on a sphere.
10. Dim.
13. Undergo something unpleasant.

Down (continued)

14. Jammed or caught.
16. Located above another part.

Mystery Letter: C

Score: /20

4

©2006. Stephen Curran

vain	plain	Word Bank
obtain	faint	TOTAL
thunder	peal	1,420
stuck	struck	

Exercise 71a

1) A bolt of lightning ___struck___ the tree and it burst into flames.

2) The fire had died down and she used the ___poker___ to stir the coals.

3) "If you listen very carefully you can hear a very ___faint___ sound of music."

4) The moth continued to ___flutter___ around inside the lampshade.

5) My sister ___rode___ her bicycle to school every day last week.

6) The bus driver asked us to use the ___upper___ deck as the lower deck was full.

7) The heavens opened and there was a ___sudden___ downpour of rain.

8) The instructions were very ___plain___ and easy to understand.

9) The bell-ringers had practised a new ___peal___ for the wedding.

10) He told them a ___joke___ and they all laughed.   **Score** [/10]

Exercise 71b

11) "Using this ___globe___ of the Earth, find the Caspian Sea."

12) He tried in ___vain___ to turn off the tap but the water continued to pour out.

13) The door was firmly ___stuck___ closed and refused to open.

14) If she did manage to open the door, it would be impossible to ___offer___ it again.

15) The lightning flashed and we counted the seconds until we heard the ___thunder___ .

16) Tickets were hard to find but we managed to ___obtain___ a pair for the final.

17) "Let us ___close___ for the victims of the disaster," said the minister.

18) I hope they did not ___suffer___ too much before they were rescued.

19) He ___play___ the organ in church every Sunday.

20) Their ___plays___ was accepted and they bought the house.   **Score** [/10]

© 2006 Stephen Curran

5

Exercise 72a

1) Many charities continue the __pocket__ to relieve suffering in the world.

2) "The doctor is very busy but he __might__ be able to see you on Thursday morning."

3) She threaded the __needle__ and began to darn his socks.

4) A beautiful multi-coloured __silver__ arced across the sky after it had rained.

5) Using a tractor and plough, the farmer turned over the __soil__ in the field.

6) The __noise__ from the racing cars was so loud that we had to wear ear defenders.

7) He used the negative to __print__ four copies of the photograph.

8) She pressed the __button__ to select the right programme on the dishwasher.

9) The __soil__ cutlery was tarnished and needed to be polished.

10) The Queen was in the parlour eating bread and __honey__ .

Score 10

Exercise 72b

11) He was old and his __sew__ was failing so he used a magnifying glass to read.

12) The electric current was still on and he received a nasty __burst__ .

13) Their office lost no time and issued a __swift__ denial of the charges.

14) It was a shame to __spoil__ their fun but it was time to go home.

15) At the weekends the boys washed cars to earn extra __money__ money.

16) She had been taught to __sight__ by her mother and knew many different stitches.

17) He had saved __moment__ by buying two for the price of one.

18) Dusk was falling and she turned on the __light__ in the hall.

19) "I shan't be long. I'll be with you in just a __sight__ ."

20) The pipe __burst__ and gallons of water flooded the kitchen.

Score 10

needle	**button**
sew	**print**
light	**sight**
might	**fight**

Word Bank TOTAL 1,440

Across

72

3. Damage or ruin something.
5. Top layer of land.
6. Sweet sticky substance made by bees.
8. Something surprising or upsetting.
12. Multicoloured arc in the sky.
13. Moving fast.
15. Split or break suddenly.
17. A sewing tool.
18. Ability to see using the eyes.
19. Mark pressed into something.

Down

1. Great power or influence.
2. Coins and banknotes.
3. Shiny metallic element.
4. A small pouch in clothes.
7. A violent encounter.
9. Not heavy.
10. A very short period of time.
11. Unpleasant sound.
14. Disc for holding clothes together.
16. Work with needle and thread.

Mystery Letter e

Score /20

stockings   high   sigh
fright   robber   ladder
bottom   rabbit   real
deal   steal   leap

Across

73

1. Pair of tightly fitting leg coverings for women.
3. Small burrowing furry mammal with long ears and short tail.
4. Of great height.
5. Sweet juicy fruit, usually with a green skin.
6. Jump over an obstacle.
9. Someone who steals.
12. Device with rungs to climb on.
14. Malicious desire to harm or humiliate.
15. Lowest part.
17. Damage by using or rubbing.

Down

1. Take unlawfully.
2. Breathe long and loud.
3. Not imaginary.
5. Pleased and satisfied.
7. Feeling of superiority.
8. Distribution of playing cards.
10. Hold the weight of something heavy.
11. Sudden fear.
13. Extreme anger.
16. Single drop of fluid from the eye.

Mystery Letter

Score /20

proud	pride
spite	rage
bear	wear
tear	pear

**Word Bank
TOTAL
1,460**

Exercise 73a

1) He was a craftsman and took great _____ in the quality of his work.

2) Susan was very _____ when she received her certificate.

3) The grizzly _____ was angry and rose up on its hind legs.

4) She took a _____ and bit into it. It was ripe and tasted very sweet.

5) Dad borrowed a friend's _____ when he painted the outside of our house.

6) The children put out _____ on Christmas Eve.

7) Everyone called him Gus but his _____ name was Angus.

8) At the very _____ of the hill the rainwater had formed a large puddle.

9) The loud noise had given her a _____ and she was still trembling.

10) She refused the offer of a lift in _____ of the cold.

Score ⟋ 10

Exercise 73b

11) Although he had outgrown his favourite jacket, he continued to _____ it.

12) He could feel his _____ mounting as he struggled to keep his temper.

13) She tried hard not to cry but a single _____ ran down her cheek.

14) He had used the opportunity to _____ the watch but he had been found out.

15) No one could see over the _____ wall that surrounded the garden.

16) She did not think she could _____ the ditch but she jumped it successfully.

17) The policeman chased the _____ who stole the handbag.

18) With a deep _____ he sank into the chair and put his head in his hands.

19) They struck a good _____ from which they both benefitted.

20) He had an Angora _____ with long silky hair.

Score ⟋ 10

singing	bringing	blowing
feeling	begin	began
begun	music	prince
princess	crown	crowd

Exercise 74a

1) The sky clouded over and it _____begun_____ to snow.

2) He increased his speed in an attempt to _____ on the leader.

3) Every __pea__ that she shelled from the pods are a rich green colour and sweet to taste.

4) The structure had __music__ to shake violently and eventually it collapsed.

5) The __state__ of the manor employed many workers on his estate.

6) A large __crowd__ had gathered to watch the display.

7) Last Christmas we went out carol _____ to collect money for charity.

8) The farmer started to __sow__ his crops early in the morning.

9) He was shivering with a temperature and __feeling__ very unwell.

10) The __grain__ in the wood looked really good when stained. **Score** [/ 10]

Exercise 74b

11) When the __wheat__ was ripe and dry it was ready to be harvested.

12) The __prince__ rode in the royal coach with his father, the King.

13) The __princess__ rode in the carriage with her mother the Queen.

14) After his death Sir Winston Churchill was honoured with a __state__ funeral.

15) "I am waiting to __begin__ the lesson but I will not start until you are all quiet."

16) The wind was __blowing__ very strongly and the trees were leaning over.

17) The _____ reached a crescendo just before the symphony ended.

18) The dentist fitted a _____ and his broken tooth looked as good as new.

19) The _____ had to be repaired and we had no gas for two days.

20) "Are you __bringing__ anyone with you to the party?" **Score** [/ 10]

10 © 2006 Stephen Curran

Across

74

3. Coming with somebody or something.
6. Sending a stream of air out from the mouth.
9. Female pig.
11. Large group of people.
12. Son of a monarch.
16. Past tense of 'begin'.
17. Performing songs.
18. Sense of touch.

Down

1. Acquire something earned.
2. Monarch's daughter or his son's wife.
3. To start.
4. Sounds played or arranged to create a pleasing effect.

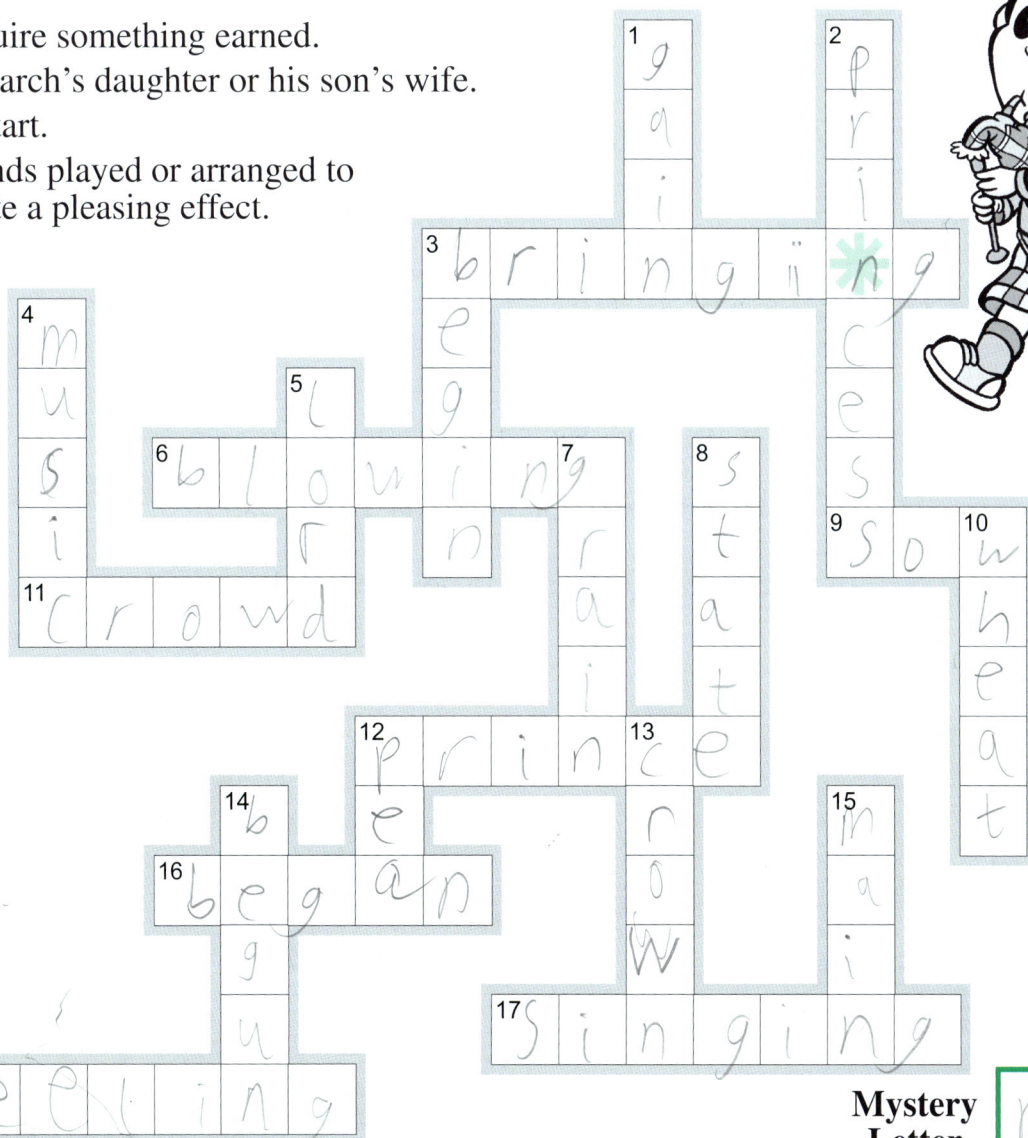

Down (continued)

5. Male member of the nobility.
7. Cereal crops.
8. Condition.
10. Grass with edible grain.
12. Round, edible, green seed that grows in a pod.
13. Headdress symbolising royalty.
14. Had started.
15. Greatest in size or importance.

Score / **20**

Mystery Letter n

Word list

turnip   straw   claw
drawing   vine   wine
grape   field   depart
travel   return   remain

Across

2. Harbour where boats or ships can dock.
5. Stay behind or wait.
8. Climbing plant.
9. Medium-sized nonhuman primate.
10. Animal's sharp nail.
11. Come or go back.
12. Stalks of threshed cereal crops.
14. To move by momentum without applying power.
17. Outline picture.
18. Alcoholic drink made from grapes.
19. Edible green or purple berry that grows in bunches.
20. Set off.

75

Down

1. Animal of the horse family with grey or brown coat, long ears and a large head.
3. Go on a journey.
4. A land mammal other than a human.
6. Plural of 'monkey'.
7. To prop up a structure.
13. Plant with large white edible root.
15. Rise and fall of the sea.
16. Area used to grow crops or graze livestock.

Mystery Letter: i

Score: 20

animal   donkey
monkey   monkeys
port   tide
shore   coast

Word Bank
TOTAL
1,500

Exercise 75a

1) The artist was _____ da drawing a portrait of his subject with pen and ink.

2) The _____ monkeys were chasing each other and swinging from the trees.

3) He switched off the engine and let the car _____ to a gradual stop.

4) The quality of the _____ grape determines the quality of the wine.

5) A _____ grape is a root vegetable whose Latin name is 'brassica rapa'.

6) The left side of a ship as you face forwards is the _____ side.

7) The sea _____ tide was littered with jetsam after the storm.

8) The ferry was scheduled to _____ from the quay at 14.30hrs.

9) The announcement told the passengers to _____ return in their seats.

10) The neap _____ occurs twice a month.

Score [/ 10]

Exercise 75b

11) Heavy rain had stripped the ripened grapes from the _____ .

12) The prize bull was a magnificent _____ and a perfect specimen.

13) His _____ was carrying a heavy load and was being led by a small boy.

14) My father's favourite _____ is Rioja which comes from Spain.

15) They paid extra to _____ first class and in extra comfort.

16) He used his bare hands to _____ his way out of the rubble.

17) His mother left a message and he used his mobile phone to _____ her call.

18) Bales of _____ were placed around the track to protect the riders if they fell.

19) "Don't be so rude you cheeky _____ !"

20) Over the hedgerow we could see the cows in the _____ .

Score [/ 10]

prison	pardon	forgive
punish	lion	rude
swan	polite	gather
rather	path	enter

Exercise 76a

1) He was found guilty of the offence and sent to _____ for eighteen months.

2) "I'd much _____ play football than stay indoors and watch television."

3) His neighbour let him _____ his ladder provided he returned it later that day.

4) The _____ is often referred to as 'the king of the jungle'.

5) Volcanoes erupt when magma bursts through the earth's _____.

6) Robin Hood fired an _____ from his bow and shot the soldier in the arm.

7) The _____ swam along majestically followed by its three cygnets.

8) He sneezed very loudly. "_____ me," he said apologetically.

9) It was very dark and from deep within the woods came the hoot of an _____.

10) He continued to _____ his opponent with body blows.   **Score** ⬜ 10

Exercise 76b

11) She was filled with _____ at the sudden loss of her dear friend.

12) He tried to _____ the building but the doors were locked securely.

13) She walked along a _____ street which was not wide enough for a car.

14) A fox had got into the coop and killed a _____.

15) The dog bared its teeth and gave a low, hostile _____.

16) She was very _____, always remembering to say "please" and "thank you".

17) "I'm sorry I forgot your birthday. Please _____ me."

18) It was a long walk but the _____ finally led to the cliff top.

19) It was milking time and the cows began to _____ at the gate.

20) It is very _____ to push in and not to wait your turn.   **Score** ⬜ 10

owl   growl
chicken   crust
arrow   narrow
sorrow   borrow

Word Bank TOTAL 1,520

Across

76

3. Big wild predatory cat.
4. Place where criminals are confined.
7. Well-mannered.
9. Ill-mannered.
10. Small in width.
12. Somewhat.
14. Hooting bird of prey.
15. Trodden track.
17. Stop resenting somebody.
18. Common domestic fowl raised for meat or eggs.

Down

1. Make a hostile sound.
2. Deep sadness or grief.
4. Forgive somebody for wrongdoing.
5. Missile shot from a bow.
6. Use somebody else's property.
8. Go or come into a place.
11. Outer part of bread.
13. Collect ideas or data.
15. Make somebody undergo a penalty.
16. Large, long-necked, white aquatic bird.

Score / **20**

Mystery Letter

15

yellow	pillow	understand
understood	shallow	stream
moss	carpet	anger
hunger	hungry	drank

Exercise 77a

1) The road had flooded and they had to _____ through deep water.

2) "I'm so _____ I could eat a horse!"

3) The glass of red wine that she dropped on the _____ had stained it badly.

4) He lifted the stone and a _____ slithered out from under it.

5) It is very dangerous to dive into the _____ end of a swimming pool.

6) Her head was too low and she asked for another _____ for her bed.

7) He would always _____ a bottle of ketchup before opening it.

8) The bright _____ of the buttercups contrasted with the green grass.

9) Her dive was almost perfect and she made hardly a _____ .

10) She was ill with a fever and her skin looked very _____ .

Score [/ 10]

Exercise 77b

11) _____ grew on the damp and shady side of the wall.

12) I tried to explain and make him _____ but he still seemed confused.

13) The water from the _____ was cool and clear and quenched his thirst.

14) He had not realised he was in any _____ until he found that he was trapped.

15) The mayor of the French town wore a red, white and blue _____ across his chest.

16) It was a wet Saturday with very few shoppers and _____ was poor.

17) He had not eaten for many hours and his _____ was growing.

18) Until you told me, I had not _____ just how much it meant to you.

19) She _____ coffee at breakfast and tea in the afternoon.

20) We really had annoyed him and his _____ was obvious.

Score [/ 10]

Word Bank TOTAL 1,540

pale   shake
snake   danger
wade   trade
sash   splash

Across

1. Past tense of *'understand'*.
4. Walk in water.
5. Not deep.
6. Simple nonflowering plant *(bryophyte)*.
8. Need for food.
9. Buying and selling.
14. A cushion for the head in bed.

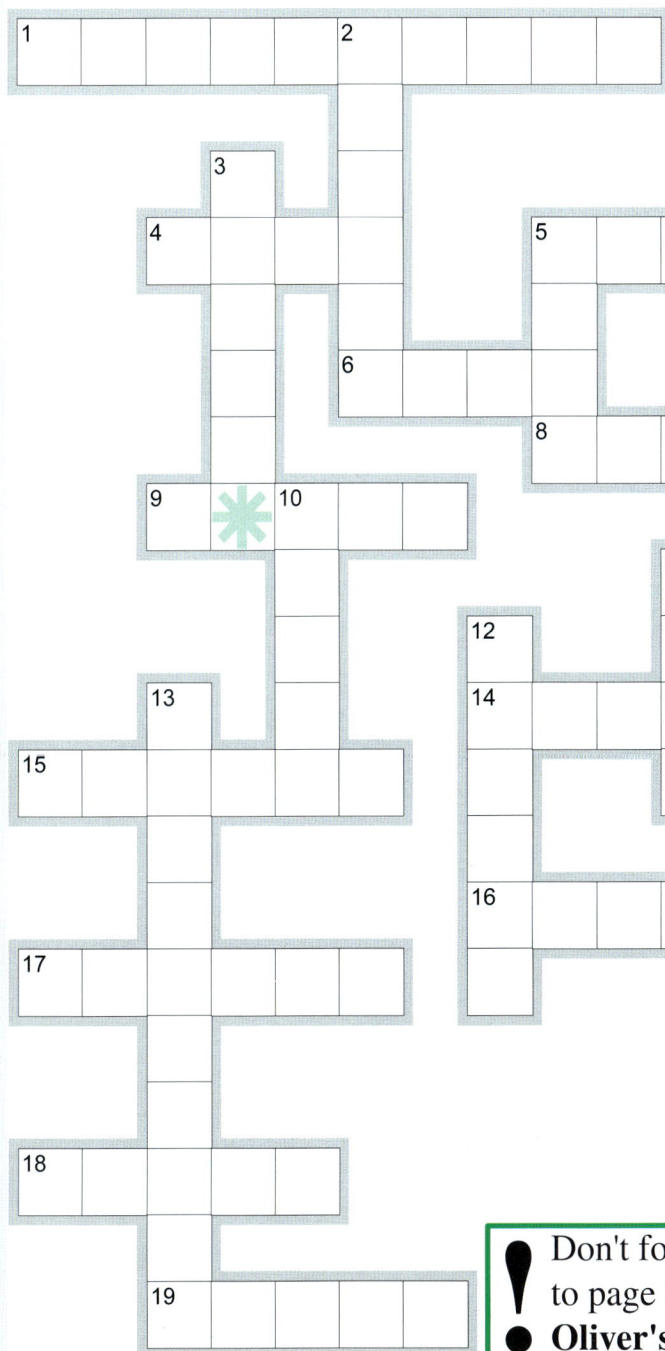

Across (continued)

15. Wanting to eat.
16. Legless reptile.
17. Thick fabric for covering a floor.
18. To tremble uncontrollably.
19. Past tense of *'drink'*.

Down

2. Constant flow.
3. Exposure to harm.
5. Wide ribbon worn across the chest.
7. The colour of butter or ripe lemons.
10. Great annoyance.
11. Lacking colour.
12. Spatter liquid.
13. Grasp the meaning of something.

! Don't forget to go back to page **3** and complete **Oliver's Mystery Word**.

Mystery Letter

Score

20

In the Bedroom

Can you find all these words in the picture below? Write the correct word against each number.

pillow	hanger	headboard	dolls' house	mirror
poster	lamp	drawer	rug	toy box
mobile	stool	alarm clock	wardrobe	slippers

1._____ 2._____ 3._____

4._____ 5._____ 6._____

7._____ 8._____ 9._____

10._____ 11._____ 12._____

13._____ 14._____ 15._____

At the Petrol Station

Can you find all these words in the picture below? Write the correct word against each number When you have finished you can colour in the picture if you want to.

petrol pump   **carwash**   **tanker**   **bonnet**   **extinguisher**
aerial   **hose**   **water**   **wing mirror**   **charcoal**
canopy   **nozzle**   **windscreen**   **watering can**   **bucket**

1._____ 2._____ 3._____

4._____ 5._____ 6._____

7._____ 8._____ 9._____

10._____ 11._____ 12._____

13._____ 14._____ 15._____

© 2006 Stephen Curran

stove   glove   cover
shelter   climb   steady
none   become   brain
brow   chest   cheek

Exercise 80a

1) She _____ on her jumper over her head.

2) He challenged the Count to a duel by slapping his face with his _____ .

3) She mopped the patient's _____ with a wet flannel.

4) The sow gave a grunt and _____ onto her side so her piglets could suckle.

5) A coal-fired _____ in the corner heated the little Victorian waiting room.

6) The ship sailed out to sea until it had _____ just a dot on the horizon.

7) The baby was wailing and tears were _____ down her cheeks.

8) The boxer's corner conceded the bout and threw the _____ into the ring.

9) He watched the squirrel _____ up the tree trunk and sit on a branch.

10) He could hear her _____ heartbeat through his stethoscope.

Score ◪ **10**

Exercise 80b

11) The tiles had been removed and a tarpaulin had been used to _____ the roof.

12) The military coup overthrew the government and seized _____ .

13) It was a very serious accident but fortunately _____ of the passengers was hurt.

14) The size of a dinosaur's _____ was tiny in relation to the size of its body.

15) The _____ kept them dry while they waited for the bus to come.

16) At the sound of the drum _____ , everyone stood to sing the national anthem.

17) Her mother kissed her on the _____ , tucked her in and said goodnight.

18) He had just come out of the _____ and had a towel around his waist.

19) An efficient use of land is to house people in _____ blocks.

20) The gorilla beat its _____ with its fists.

Score ◪ **10**

© 2006 Stephen Curran

Exercise 81a

1) Bonfire night on 5th _____ commemorates the Gunpowder Plot of 1605.

2) The newly dug _____ greatly improved the irrigation of the field.

3) The doctor's surgery was full but _____ was seen eventually.

4) American Independence Day is celebrated on 4th _____ .

5) The cricketers shouted " _____ !" and the batsman was out: caught and bowled.

6) His trousers were old and worn and had a large _____ sewn on one knee.

7) He was a very _____ professor and taught at Oxford University.

8) After being at sea for weeks, they finally _____ the safety of dry land.

9) "Can you _____ my cardigan from upstairs?" asked Granddad. "I'm cold."

10) The new school year begins in _____ .

Score ⬜ /10

Exercise 81b

11) It was a very pretty _____ with a thatched roof and roses round the door.

12) We _____ the strawberries, had them weighed and paid for them at the till.

13) He was no _____ for his tennis opponent and was beaten in straight sets.

14) The summer solstice falls on 24th _____ and is known as Midsummer Day.

15) Summer _____ is made from stewed fresh fruit and slices of bread.

16) He looked at his _____ and noted that it was seven o'clock.

17) He used the time between flights to _____ a few minutes of sleep.

18) The task was much bigger than she had imagined and she was losing _____ .

19) The lorry was running downhill and _____ up speed.

20) She had to seize the moment and _____ very quickly.

Score ⬜ /10

care	careless	useless
useful	infant	darling
cradle	young	tender
gentle	weak	dull

Exercise 82a

1) The hacksaw _____ was very blunt so he changed it for a new one.

2) A sharp axe is safer and more efficient to use than one that is _____ .

3) The polar bear's thick coat of white _____ keeps him warm in the Arctic weather.

4) "Take _____ when crossing the road," the mother told her daughter.

5) She placed her new baby in the _____ and gently rocked him to sleep.

6) His card read: 'To my _____ wife with love on our wedding anniversary'.

7) She was very _____ and often knocked things over.

8) The steak was so _____ he had no trouble cutting it.

9) She took her _____ out of her handbag and paid the bill.

10) Swiss army knives have many really _____ tools.

Score [/10]

Exercise 82b

11) The children watched the blacksmith _____ the horseshoe into shape.

12) _____ schools are for children between the ages of four and seven.

13) The hill was not steep: there was a _____ incline down to the stream.

14) Two old men were sitting in the sunshine on the _____ beside the river.

15) The bridge had been badly damaged and was too _____ to carry traffic.

16) The blackbird had a large worm in its _____ .

17) Her umbrella kept blowing inside out and was _____ in the high winds.

18) The workman used a _____ brush to remove the rust from the railings.

19) He was only sixteen years old and too _____ to drive a car.

20) The doctor asked the _____ to dress the patient's wounds.

Score [/10]

purse   nurse
fur   beak
hammer   bench
blade   wire

Word Bank TOTAL 1,640

Across

82

1. Blunt and lacking the ability to cut cleanly.
3. Not very old.
5. Baby's bed.
8. Very young child that can neither walk nor talk.
9. Hand tool for driving in nails.
11. Sharp-edged cutting part of a tool or weapon.
13. Unusable.
15. Not fit or strong.
16. Unusually sensitive when touched or pressed.

Down

1. Form of address to a loved one.
2. Mammal's soft dense coat of hair.
4. Serving a purpose.
5. Disregarding or showing no concern.
6. Long backless seat without arms.
7. To be interested or concerned.
10. Small bag for carrying personal money.
11. Bird's horny mouth.
12. Having a mild and kind nature.
14. Somebody caring for patients.
15. Strand of metal.

Mystery Letter

Score / 20

too	tool	stool
fool	lunch	buy
beef	cloth	blood
goose	geese	cheese

Across

83

1. No longer whole.
4. Acquire something by payment.
5. Past tense of *'steal'*.
6. As well.
7. Plural of *'goose'*.
9. Fabric made by weaving, knitting, or felting thread or fibres.
10. Period taken away from an activity for a rest, change, or meal.
11. Device for doing work.
12. Meat from cattle.

Across (continued)

13. Became or made different.
15. Past participle of *'take'*.
16. A shift from one state, stage, or phase to another.

Down

1. Past tense of *'break'*.
2. Midday meal.
3. Unintelligent or thoughtless person.
7. Large waterfowl noted for its seasonal migrations and distinctive honking sound.
8. Simple seat with three or four legs with no back or arm rests.
9. Solid food made from milk.
10. Red fluid circulating around the body.
14. Consumed as sustenance.

Mystery Letter

Score

/20

change   changed
taken   eaten
break   broke
broken   stole

Word Bank TOTAL 1,660

Exercise 83a

1) She wore an evening dress and had a white _____ across her shoulders.

2) The chemistry laboratory had long benches with a _____ for each pupil to sit on.

3) A typical English Sunday lunch is roast _____ served with Yorkshire puddings.

4) _____ is eaten in the middle of the day and dinner is eaten in the evening.

5) When they returned from America they _____ $200 back into Sterling.

6) A flock of migrating _____ flew over honking loudly.

7) They went to a different restaurant in which they had not _____ before.

8) "I'm _____ because I've spent all my pocket money on sweets."

9) "We're going to the beach today and, if you like, you can come _____."

10) Muslin is a thin, plain-weave, cotton _____ .

Score [/ 10]

Exercise 83b

11) I like Cheddar and Wensleydale but my favourite _____ is Camembert.

12) The eggs of a _____ are larger than those of a chicken.

13) The tyre had punctured and the AA patrol man had to _____ the wheel.

14) She had _____ her promise to keep the secret and now everyone knew.

15) She had _____ great care not to wake him when she entered the room.

16) Septicaemia is a disease caused by microorganisms in the _____ .

17) "Simon, act sensibly for once and do not _____ around during the lesson!"

18) He took the mower and the edging shears out of the _____ shed and cut the lawn.

19) Sharon had just enough money left to _____ herself an ice cream.

20) Huge waves continued to _____ over the rocks.

Score [/ 10]

wrath	wrestling	writhe
wrapper	wreckage	wren
wristwatch	fudge	hedgehog
sledge	neigh	weird

Exercise 84a

1) He adjusted his new _____ to show the correct time and date.

2) The young _____ was sick and had to be separated from the other cows.

3) Chemists and cooks use a pestle and _____ to grind substances into a powder.

4) During laboratory experiments we always wear _____ to protect our eyes.

5) Whenever you finish a chocolate bar always throw the _____ into a bin.

6) Dad got our _____ out of the loft so we could ride it downhill on the snow.

7) The tiny _____ was startled and flew away before I could photograph it.

8) The racehorse was injured and the jockey decided to _____ it in.

9) "The steps are very steep so use the _____ to help you climb."

10) Gymnasts use a _____ to improve their vaults.   **Score** [/10]

Exercise 84b

11) It was a wealthy _____ full of large detached houses.

12) The marauders incurred the _____ of the villagers who then sought vengeance.

13) The sound of a horse's _____ came from the stables.

14) The _____ felt threatened and curled itself into a tight prickly ball.

15) A fence _____ had been broken by the high winds and needed replacing.

16) The plane crashed in the mountains and _____ covered a wide area.

17) The policeman was _____ with the man and trying to restrain him.

18) It was a _____ feeling and it was as if she were floating on water.

19) He had tried to _____ the results by altering the figures.

20) He held up the snake and watched it _____ in his hand.   **Score** [/10]

Word Bank

needle   button
sew   print
light   sight
might   fight

Word Bank TOTAL 1,440

Across

3. Damage or ruin something.
5. Top layer of land.
6. Sweet sticky substance made by bees.
8. Something surprising or upsetting.
12. Multicoloured arc in the sky.
13. Moving fast.
15. Split or break suddenly.
17. A sewing tool.
18. Ability to see using the eyes.
19. Mark pressed into something.

Down

1. Great power or influence.
2. Coins and banknotes.
3. Shiny metallic element.
4. A small pouch in clothes.
7. A violent encounter.
9. Not heavy.
10. A very short period of time.
11. Unpleasant sound.
14. Disc for holding clothes together.
16. Work with needle and thread.

Mystery Letter: e

Score: 20

Across

73

1. Pair of tightly fitting leg coverings for women.
3. Small burrowing furry mammal with long ears and short tail.
4. Of great height.
5. Sweet juicy fruit, usually with a green skin.
6. Jump over an obstacle.
9. Someone who steals.
12. Device with rungs to climb on.
14. Malicious desire to harm or humiliate.
15. Lowest part.
17. Damage by using or rubbing.

Down

1. Take unlawfully.
2. Breathe long and loud.
3. Not imaginary.
5. Pleased and satisfied.
7. Feeling of superiority.
8. Distribution of playing cards.
10. Hold the weight of something heavy.
11. Sudden fear.
13. Extreme anger.
16. Single drop of fluid from the eye.

Mystery Letter

Score 20

8

Across

84

4. Flexible diving board.
5. Mixture of sand, cement and water to join and hold bricks together.
7. A type of soft toffee.
10. Fury often marked by a desire for vengeance.
12. Young cow.
13. Small vehicle for sliding over snow.
14. A local community.
17. Fight by gripping and pushing.
18. A watch on a band or strap worn around the wrist.
19. Group of judges or speakers.

Down

1. Small brown songbird.
2. The remains after destruction.
3. Material wrapped around something.
6. Small spiny animal.
8. Protective glasses fitting tight to the face.
9. Long high-pitched horse sound.
10. Strange or unusual.
11. A rail for holding onto.
15. Strap for controlling a horse.
16. Twist or squirm in agony.

Don't forget to go back to page **21** and complete **Kate's Mystery Word**.

Mystery Letter

Score
20

33

In the Kitchen

Can you find all these words in the picture below? Write the correct word against each number. When you have finished you can colour in the picture if you want to.

cereal	**fridge**	**cooker**	**saucepan**	**bread bin**
taps	**tiles**	**kettle**	**toaster**	**blind**
teapot	**mug tree**	**ladle**	**tea towel**	**socket**

1._____   2._____   3._____

4._____   5._____   6._____

7._____   8._____   9._____

10._____   11._____   12._____

13._____   14._____   15._____

At the Railway Station

Can you find all these words in the picture below? Write the correct word against each number.

footbridge	guard	signboard	carriage	porter
signal	sleeper	platform	kiosk	barrow
rail	billboard	barrier	bench	commuter

1._____ 2._____ 3._____

4._____ 5._____ 6._____

7._____ 8._____ 9._____

10._____ 11._____ 12._____

13._____ 14._____ 15._____

STATION

ARRIVAL 08:45
DEPART 08:49

spectators	balcony	flippers
haul	gaudy	saunter
sausages	sauce	autograph
vault	mauve	draught

Exercise 85a

1) Leaves had blocked the _____ and rainwater overflowed.

2) The colour of the paint was a _____ shade of shocking pink.

3) She boiled the potatoes in a _____ and then mashed them.

4) The soldier had _____ an order and faced a court martial.

5) Seated up in the _____ they had an excellent view of the stage.

6) "Keep up with the rest of us and don't _____ along behind!"

7) She asked the player for his _____ and he wrote it on her programme.

8) Generations of their family had been buried in the underground _____ .

9) Malt is produced from _____ and is used to make beer and whisky.

10) The lepidopterist added a new _____ to his collection. **Score** ⬜/10

Exercise 85b

11) He gave the _____ the manuscript for his speech.

12) The artist painted the sky a pale _____ by mixing blue, red and white paint.

13) The sea was becoming shallower and nearing the limit for the ship's _____ .

14) A thick creamy _____ had been poured over the dessert.

15) Wearing a mask, snorkel and _____ , she was ready to explore underwater.

16) Several _____ were injured when the grandstand collapsed.

17) Before barbecuing the _____ , we pricked their skins with a fork.

18) It was only a small _____ but the trees and shrubs supported much wildlife.

19) The poached cod was served with a delicious _____ sauce.

20) It was a large _____ and the little fishing boat was full. **Score** ⬜/10

Across

85

4. People who watch or observe.
7. Aquatic animal's limbs.
12. Current of uncomfortably cold air.
15. Cereal plant grown for food and malt production.
16. To walk at an easy unhurried pace.
17. Herb of the carrot family used in cooking and as a garnish.
18. Platform on the wall of a building.
19. Pale purplish colour.

Down

1. Cooking pot with a handle.
2. Refused or failed to obey a rule, instruction, or authority.
3. Typewriter or keyboard operator.
5. Small thicket or wood.
6. Underground room with an arched ceiling.
8. Rainwater channel on a roof.
9. Somebody's signature.
10. To move something with effort.
11. Insect with two pairs of big colourful wings.

Down (continued)

13. Brightly coloured or showily decorated to an unpleasant or vulgar degree.
14. Flavouring liquid for food.
16. Spicy meat in tube-shaped casings.

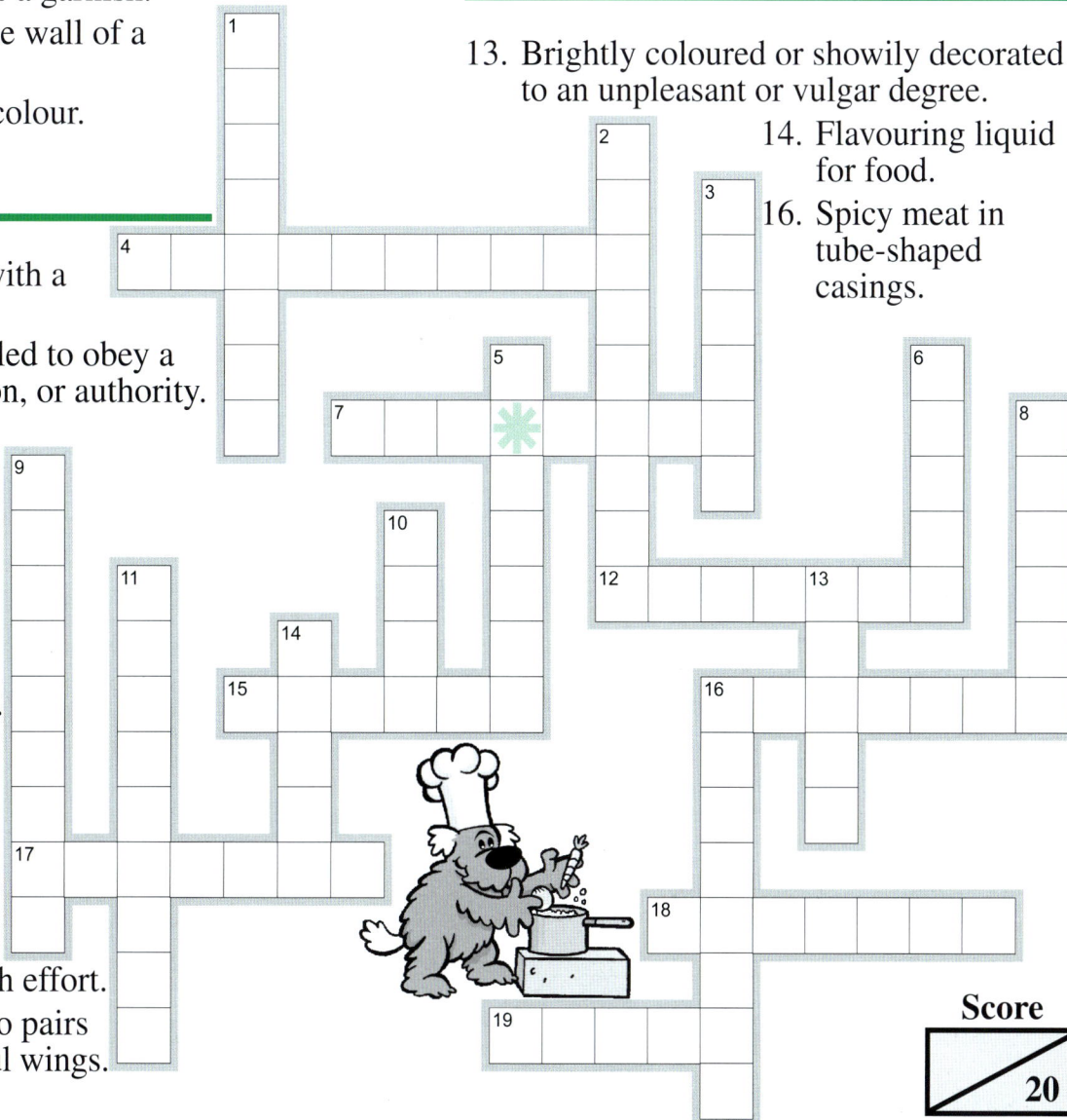

Put the mystery letters from the starred squares (✳) in puzzles **85** to **92** into their numbered box below, then rearrange them to make **Dickens's Mystery Word**. The clue is **PROFESSION**.

Score 20

Enter your mystery letters here:

85	86	87	88	89	90	91	92

Now rearrange them to make the:

Mystery Word:

© 2006 Stephen Curran

37

hyphen   magnifying   dyeing
rhyme   terrifying   syrup
rhythm   joint   oilfield
ointment   boiling   coiled

Across

86

2. Alteration that removes an error.
4. Obscured from view.
7. The yellow portion of an egg.
8. People.
10. Increasing the apparent size of something.
16. Dash to link two elements in a compound word.
17. Greasy soothing or softening substance used on the skin.
18. Oil-producing area.
19. Stand around idly.

Down

1. Extremely hot.
2. Wound into a series of connected loops.
3. Patterns of beats in music.
5. Sweet liquid made of sugar.
6. A large piece of roasted meat.
9. Containing or producing poison.
11. Book of word meanings.
12. Making somebody very frightened.
13. Similarity in the sound of word endings.
14. Fixed amount allocated to an individual.
15. Colouring something by soaking in a colouring solution.

Mystery Letter

Score
/ 20

38

loiter	yolk	Word Bank
folk	ration	TOTAL
correction	dictionary	1,720
poisonous	hidden	

Exercise 86a

1) The philatelist used his _____ glass to study the stamp.

2) The young lads, with nothing else to do, would _____ on the street corner.

3) Always use a _____ to look up the meaning of every new word.

4) Her skin was very itchy but the _____ gave some relief when rubbed on.

5) It had been _____ and she would never forget the fear that she had felt.

6) "If you are lucky, you may discover a double _____ in your egg."

7) He loved to pour a generous amount of maple _____ over his pancakes.

8) The _____ of the music was infectious and we just had to get up and dance.

9) When supplies were limited, the government had to _____ petrol.

10) The adder is the only _____ snake in Great Britain. **Score** ◻/10

Exercise 86b

11) Further exploration of the _____ had shown there was still a plentiful supply.

12) _____ point is the temperature at which a liquid turns to gas.

13) Her little brother's favourite nursery _____ was *The Grand Old Duke of York*.

14) The control tower advised the pilot to make a small _____ to his course.

15) The two of them agreed and, together, they had made a _____ decision.

16) He had tried to escape with the stolen goods _____ under his coat.

17) Before _____ her hair blonde she had always been a brunette.

18) "My name is Courteney-Jones: a double-barrelled name spelt with a _____ ."

19) On the deck all the ropes were _____ neatly.

20) Traditional _____ songs have been passed down orally. **Score** ◻/10

nodding	**grabbed**	**assembly**
passport	**pheasant**	**phantom**
murmur	**turban**	**turquoise**
quoit	**quantity**	**query**

Exercise 87a

1) The _______________ council meets at the town hall to consider local matters.

2) There appeared to be a mistake on his gas bill so he rang up to _____________ it.

3) He had to show his ________________ before passing through immigration.

4) ______________ are worn on Remembrance Day which is on 11th November.

5) He was proposing a solution and everyone was _______________ in agreement.

6) Many __________________ from around the world make up the United Nations.

7) The ____________ that fought in the First World War suffered huge losses.

8) The Indic language spoken by _____________ is called Romany.

9) She suffered from a ______________ illness whose cause could not be ascertained.

10) Sanjit is a Sikh and covers his head with a ___________ .

Score ___ / 10

Exercise 87b

11) He saw her topple forward and he ______________ her arm to stop her from falling.

12) He put all his ____________ behind him and concentrated on getting a good result.

13) The ______________ of the bride and groom celebrated the couple's wedding.

14) She wore a large pendant of greenish-blue ________________ on a gold chain.

15) William Shakespeare would have used a ___________ pen to write his plays.

16) She tried in vain to throw the ___________ over the small post a few feet away.

17) The butcher also sold game birds including ________________ and grouse.

18) There was a huge _______________ of fans at the open air concert.

19) When the concert was over there was a large ______________ of litter left behind.

20) He heard the woman quietly _____________ her disapproval.

Score ___ / 10

Across

87

2. A town with a corporation.
4. Plants with large red, orange, or white flowers and cup-shaped seed pods.
7. Continuous low sound.
8. Moving the head in agreement.
10. Ring used in the game of quoits.
11. People with a nomadic lifestyle.
14. A request for information.
15. Large organised groups of soldiers.
16. Causes of anxiety.

Across (continued)

17. Gathering of people.
18. An amount or number of something.

Down

1. Nations that are politically independent.
3. Official identification document for travelling to and from a country.
4. Unreal being or sensation.
5. Groups with something in common.
6. Greenish-blue semiprecious stone.
9. Seized violently.
12. Large long-tailed bird frequently bred for shooting.
13. Man's headdress that consists of a long piece of fabric wrapped around the head to completely cover the hair.
14. Pen made from a feather shaft.

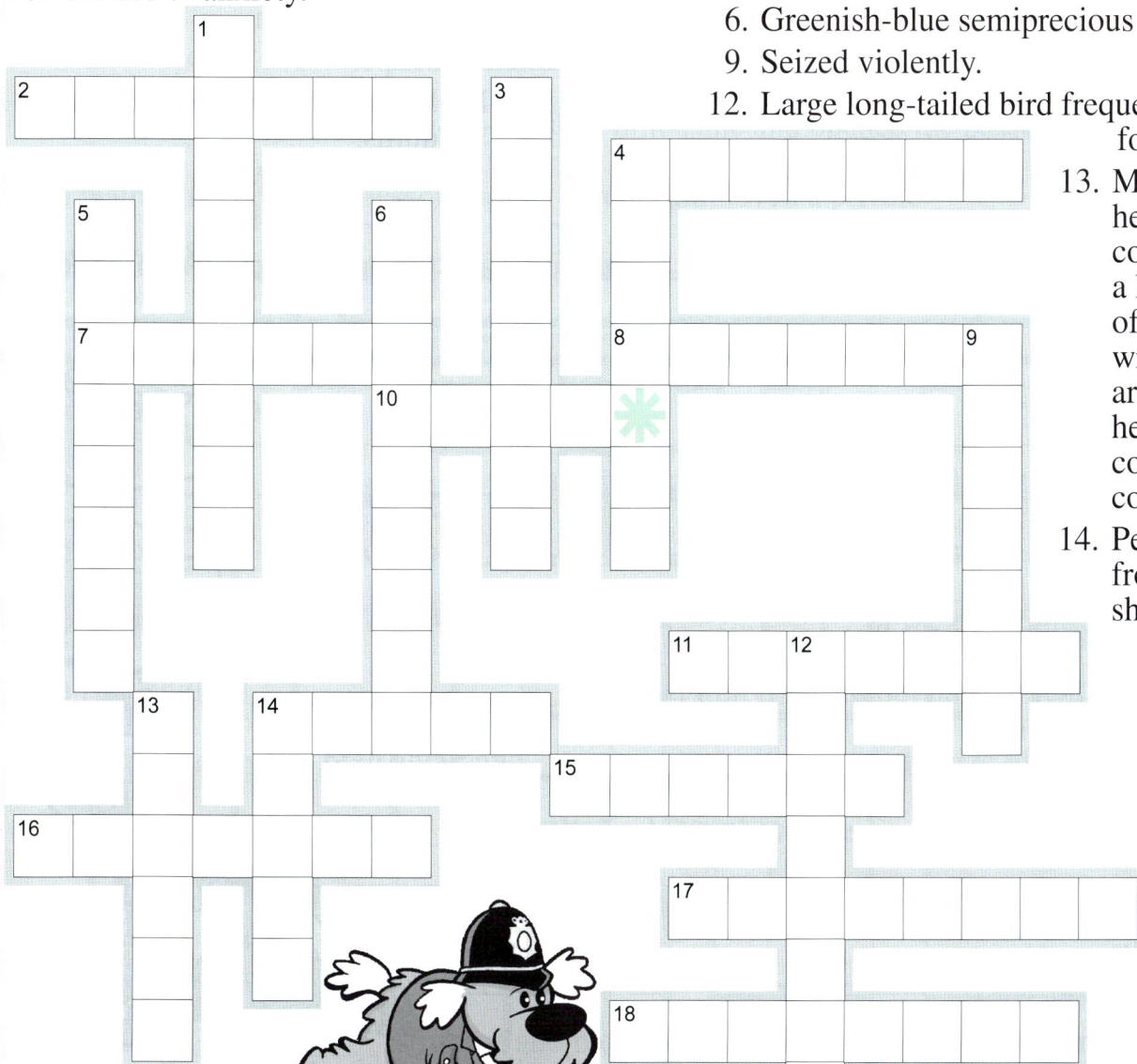

Mystery Letter

Score / 20

Across

90

3. Large pad for sleeping on.
4. Common bird with black feathers.
7. Cut food into cubes.
10. Long, flat piece of wood.
11. Stopper for a sink.
13. Mix ingredients.
15. Tests of knowledge.

Across (continued)

16. Sweet or savoury unyeasted cake usually split and buttered.
17. Music with syncopated rhythms and improvisation.
18. Lie or sit lazily.
19. Tremble with fear.

Down

1. Vehicle powered by a diesel engine.
2. Hair-cleaning soap.
4. Severe snowstorm with strong winds.
5. Electronic sound repeated intermittently.
6. Cluster of things.
8. Collapsible movable shelter.
9. Laugh lightly.
12. Meat seller.
14. Short tapered tube.

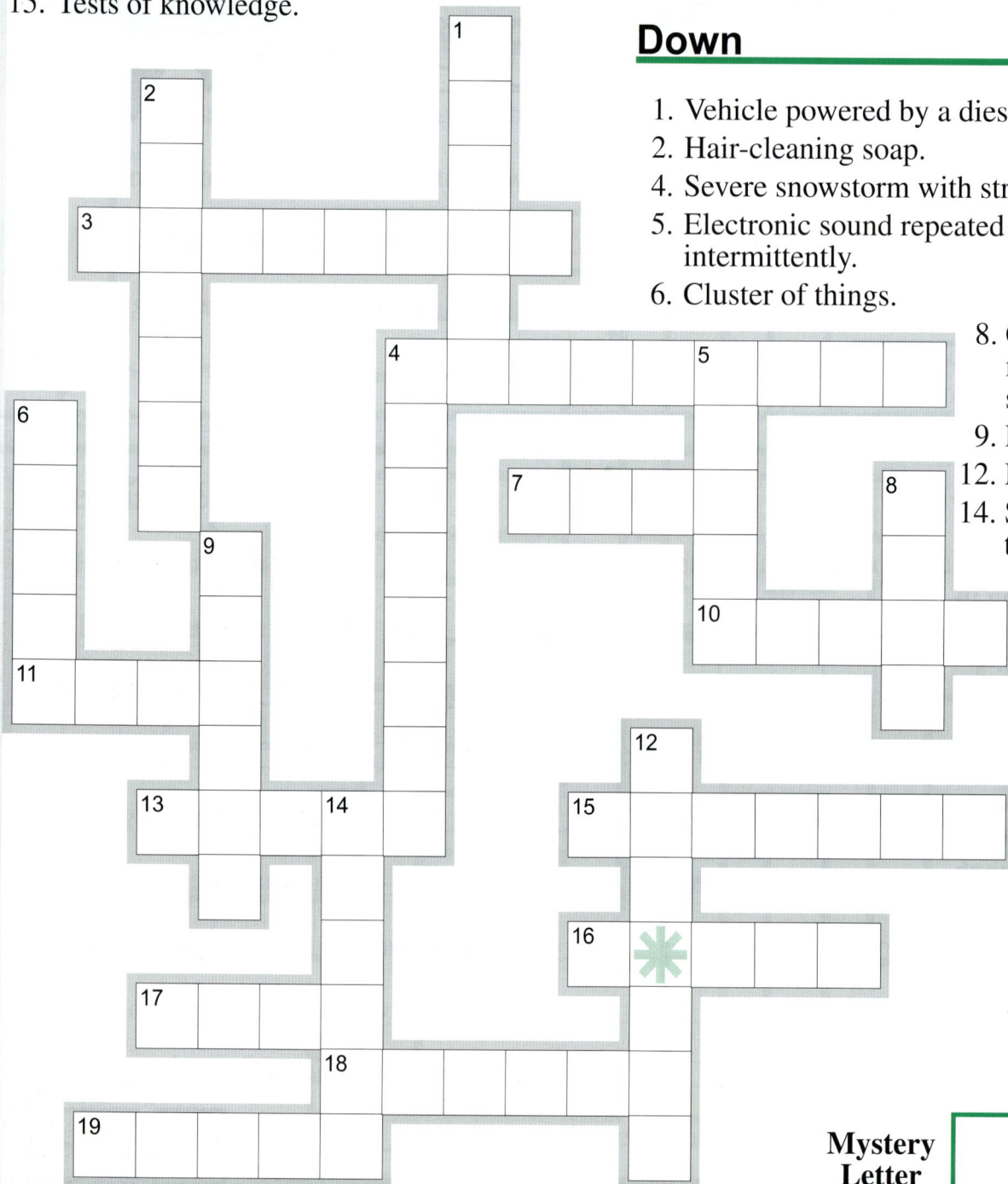

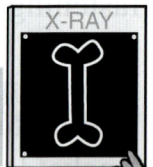

Mystery Letter

Score

/20

X-RAY

46

© 2006 Stephen Curran

Exercise 90a

1) She washed her baby's hair with a _____ that would not sting his eyes.

2) The computer started up, gave a _____ and continued to load the programs.

3) They pitched their _____ on the higher ground to avoid it being flooded.

4) There was a large _____ of moss at the base of the tree trunk.

5) The trapped animal was petrified and began to _____ with fear.

6) The _____ picked the berry and held it in its bright yellow beak.

7) The strength of the wind increased and the snowstorm became a _____ .

8) He laid down and felt the springs in the old _____ digging into his back.

9) _____ engines use less fuel per kilometre than petrol engines.

10) She put in the _____ , turned on the taps and ran a bath.   **Score** [/10]

Exercise 90b

11) One fireman held the _____ and another supported the hose behind him.

12) She used a food processor to _____ together the required ingredients.

13) Regular _____ with questions on general knowledge were held each month.

14) _____ music is characterised by syncopated rhythms and improvisation.

15) She loved to hear her toddler _____ whenever something amused him.

16) She cut the warm _____ in two and spread both halves with butter.

17) He was a _____ . He wore an apron and used a cleaver to cut joints of meat.

18) They needed a large _____ of wood to repair the deck of the ship.

19) "Please go through to the _____ and take a seat on the sofa."

20) "Double six! Throw the _____ again."   **Score** [/10]

mammal	panda	sculpture
walkers	squat	buzzard
buzz	scruffy	drip
scroll	twinge	wring

Exercise 91a

1) The thread of her _____ broke and coloured beads cascaded everywhere.

2) "_____ out your swimming things and hang them up to dry."

3) The sprinter felt a _____ from an old injury and pulled up immediately.

4) The ostrich is a two-toed African flightless bird that only _____ and runs.

5) He had climbed over the fence and _____ his trousers on the barbed wire.

6) London Zoo was looking forward to the arrival of a _____ from China.

7) Just like us, an ape is a _____ but so is a dolphin and a whale.

8) The tap needed a new washer and it continued to _____ after being turned off.

9) The oven timer gave a long _____ when it was time to take out the cake.

10) The harvesters carried the _____ of corn to the wagon.

Score ⟋ 10

Exercise 91b

11) He had honed the axe on the whetstone and it was now much _____ .

12) The friends hired a narrowboat and _____ along the canals of Britain.

13) A large _____ slowly circled above them looking for prey.

14) The pickets fought with the workers in a _____ outside the factory gates.

15) It was a very impressive _____ of the Duke of Wellington on his horse.

16) The house was very _____ and needed to be completely redecorated.

17) "Could you all _____ on the ground under that tree and rest in the shade."

18) She used the computer mouse to _____ down the pages on the internet.

19) She was wearing a new skirt and the colour really _____ her.

20) Over thirty _____ had covered the full distance.

Score ⟋ 10

Word Bank TOTAL 1,820

Across

91

1. Twist and compress something in order to force water out of it.
5. Short and solidly built.
8. More pointed.
9. Travelled by sea.
13. Large Eurasian hawk with broad wings and broad tail.
14. Torn.
17. Bundles of objects gathered or tied together.
18. Noisy fight.

Down

2. Neck ornament.
3. Large black-and-white Chinese mammal.
4. Steady humming sound like that of a bee.
5. Untidy or shabby.
6. Sudden brief stab of pain.

Down (continued)

7. Three-dimensional work of art.
8. Looked good on somebody.
10. Journeys made on foot.
11. People who walk.
12. Roll of parchment.
15. Fall as drops of liquid.
16. Class of warm-blooded vertebrate animals.

Score

Mystery Letter

/ **20**

coldest	gnaw	everybody
fluent	notch	meadow
seaside	waterproof	womb
harder	punctuation	overstretched

Exercise 92a

1) Their resources were _____ and could not cope with the situation.

2) He cut a shallow _____ in his longbow to hold the bowstring in position.

3) Descending the steps was easy, climbing back up was much _____ .

4) She opened the window to water the pot plants she kept on the _____ .

5) It was the _____ night that year with a temperature of minus eight degrees.

6) Her dog had to go into _____ when she returned from America.

7) He tried to keep up with the leaders but he just could not run any _____ .

8) At the _____ they played on the beach and walked along the promenade.

9) Dawn was breaking and it was getting _____ as the sun came up.

10) She is very _____ in both Spanish and French.

Score ◿ 10

Exercise 92b

11) My dog loves to _____ a fresh bone and extract the marrow from it.

12) Colons, commas, full stops and hyphens are all _____ marks.

13) Jessica's father decorated her bedroom and hung new _____ .

14) The crew ran to the lifeboat station and put on their _____ clothing.

15) He came from the southern United States and spoke with a slow _____ .

16) He tried to rescue the cat but it climbed up even _____ into the tree.

17) The _____ contained a large herd of brown and white Guernsey cows.

18) The scan showed a clear picture of the baby growing in her _____ .

19) "Remember, you can't please _____ all of the time!"

20) The pillow was hard and she changed it for a _____ one.

Score ◿ 10

50

© 2006 Stephen Curran

Word Bank

drawl lighter
softer higher
faster quarantine
wallpaper windowsill

Word Bank TOTAL 1,840

Across

3. Shelf on the bottom edge of a window.
6. Every person.
8. More easily shaped, bent or cut.
10. More difficult to understand or explain.
12. Marks used to organise writing.
13. Nick or indentation cut into something.
15. At the lowest temperature.
16. Acting or moving more rapidly.
17. Enforced isolation to prevent spread of disease.
19. Grassy field.

Down

1. Chew at something.
2. Of greater height.
3. Impervious to water.
4. Less heavy.
5. Area of land bordering the sea.
7. Tried to do too much with the resources available.
9. Able to speak a language with ease.
11. Speak slowly with the vowel sounds drawn out.
14. Patterned paper to decorate walls.
18. The uterus of a woman.

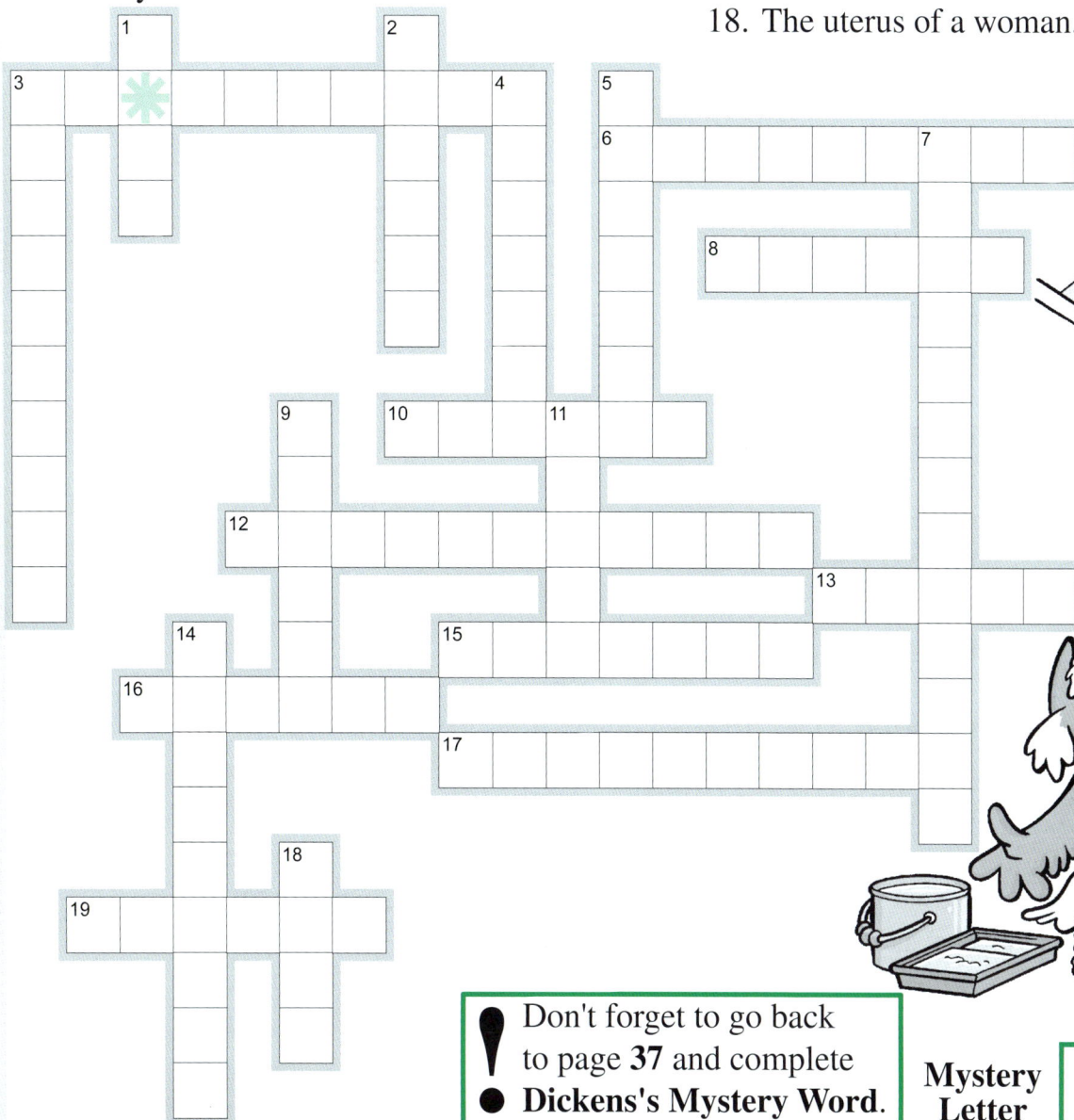

92

! Don't forget to go back to page **37** and complete ● **Dickens's Mystery Word**.

Mystery Letter

Score /20

© 2006 Stephen Curran

51

Book Four Word List

act	butterfly	deafening	fudge
almond	button	deal	fur
anger	buy	depart	gain
animal	buzz	dice	gather
anybody	buzzard	dictionary	gaudy
April	candle	diesel	geese
armies	cannot	dirty	gentle
arrow	cape	disobeyed	giggle
assembly	care	ditch	giraffe
astronaut	careless	donkey	gleam
autograph	carpet	drag	globe
balcony	catch	drank	glove
barley	chaffinch	draught	gnaw
beak	change	drawing	goggles
bear	changed	drawl	goose
become	charge	drip	grabbed
beef	chauffeur	dull	grain
began	cheek	dusty	grape
begin	cheese	dyeing	grave
begun	chest	eaten	growl
bench	chicken	enter	gutter
blackbird	chimpanzee	everybody	gypsies
blade	claw	everyone	hammer
blastoff	climb	exaggerate	handle
bleep	close	faint	handrail
blend	cloth	families	handsaw
blizzard	cloudy	faster	happen
blood	clump	feathers	harder
blowing	coast	feeling	haul
boiling	coiled	fetch	heart
borough	coldest	field	hedgehog
borrow	comb	fight	heifer
bottom	correction	flamingo	helmet
brain	cottage	flippers	hidden
brawl	countries	fluent	high
break	cover	flutter	higher
bringing	cradle	folk	honey
broke	crowd	fool	hunger
broken	crown	forgive	hungry
brow	cruised	form	hyphen
buffalo	crumb	Friday	infant
burst	crust	fright	inventor
busy	danger	front	jazz
butcher	darling	frosty	jealousy

52

Book Four Word List

joint	neigh	port	saucepan
joke	neighbourhood	power	saunter
July	nobody	pray	sausages
June	nodding	pride	saying
kangaroo	noise	prince	scald
kipper	none	princess	scone
ladder	notch	print	scream
lamb	November	prison	screwdriver
large	nozzle	proud	scroll
leap	nurse	pudding	scruffy
learned	obtain	pulled	sculptor
light	offer	punctuation	sculpture
lighter	oilfield	punish	seaside
lion	ointment	purse	seniors
loiter	overstretched	quake	September
lord	owl	quantity	sew
lounge	pale	quarantine	shake
lucky	panda	query	shallow
lunch	panel	quill	shampoo
magnifying	pardon	quizzes	shape
main	parsley	quoit	sharper
mallet	passport	rabbit	shave
mammal	patch	rage	sheaves
marble	path	rainbow	shelter
March	paying	rather	shock
match	pea	ration	shore
mattress	peal	reached	shower
mauve	pear	real	shuffle
May	phantom	rein	sigh
meadow	pheasant	remain	sight
might	picked	return	silver
moment	picking	rhinoceros	singing
Monday	pillow	rhododendron	skateboard
money	plain	rhyme	slave
monkey	plank	rhythm	sledge
monkeys	playing	ripped	sleepy
month	plays	robber	snake
mortar	plug	rode	snatch
moss	pocket	roll	softer
murmur	poisonous	rolled	soil
music	poker	rolling	someone
narrow	polite	rude	something
necklace	poppies	sash	sometimes
needle	porcupine	sauce	sorrow

Book Four Word List

sort	stuck	ton	walks
sow	sudden	too	wallpaper
spectators	suffer	tool	watch
spinney	suited	towel	waterproof
spite	Sunday	tower	weak
splash	surgeon	trade	wear
spoil	surgery	travel	weasel
sport	surname	treat	weird
springboard	surplice	trust	wheat
squat	surrounded	tumble	windowsill
stable	surveyor	turban	wine
state	survivor	turnip	wire
staying	swan	turquoise	womb
steady	swift	tutor	won
steal	syrup	twinge	wonder
stealthily	taken	typist	worries
steam	team	understand	wrapper
stockings	tear	understood	wrath
stole	tender	unless	wreckage
stool	tent	upper	wren
stormy	terrifying	useful	wrestling
stove	thorn	useless	wring
strange	threatened	vain	wristwatch
stranger	thumb	vault	writhe
straw	thunder	vine	yellow
stream	Thursday	wade	yolk
struck	tide	walkers	young

Congratulations!

You have now learnt to spell **1,840** words, know what they mean and how to use them in a sentence.

Now move on to **Book 5** to learn lots more words to add to your word bank total.

Exercise 70a

1) Monday
2) shape
3) playing
4) gleam
5) team
6) month
7) cape
8) staying
9) wonder
10) scream

Exercise 70b

11) steam
12) front
13) treat
14) saying
15) grave
16) shave
17) ton
18) won
19) slave
20) paying

Exercise 71a

1) struck
2) poker
3) faint
4) flutter
5) rode
6) upper
7) sudden
8) plain
9) peal
10) joke

Exercise 71b

11) globe
12) vain
13) stuck
14) close
15) thunder
16) obtain
17) pray
18) suffer
19) plays
20) offer

Exercise 72a

1) fight
2) might
3) needle
4) rainbow
5) soil
6) noise
7) print
8) button
9) silver
10) honey

Exercise 72b

11) sight
12) shock
13) swift
14) spoil
15) pocket
16) sew
17) money
18) light
19) moment
20) burst

Crossword No. 70

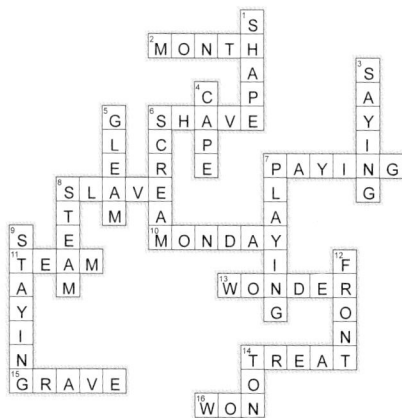

Crossword No. 71

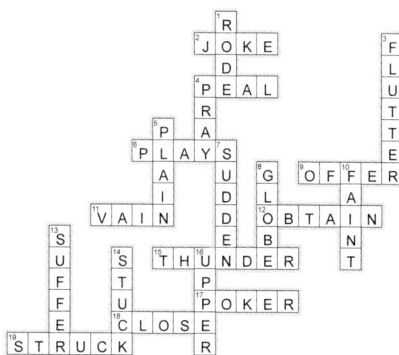

Crossword No. 72

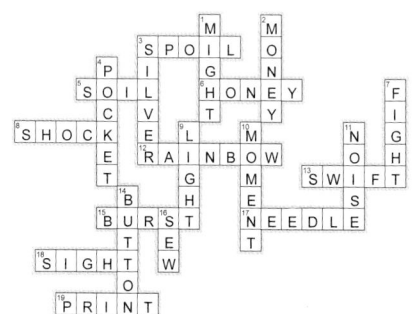

Letter = T

Letter = C

Letter = E

Answers

Exercise 73a

1) pride
2) proud
3) bear
4) pear
5) ladder
6) stockings
7) real
8) bottom
9) fright
10) spite

Exercise 73b

11) wear
12) rage
13) tear
14) steal
15) high
16) leap
17) robber
18) sigh
19) deal
20) rabbit

Exercise 74a

1) began
2) gain
3) pea
4) begun
5) lord
6) crowd
7) singing
8) sow
9) feeling
10) grain

Exercise 74b

11) wheat
12) prince
13) princess
14) state
15) begin
16) blowing
17) music
18) crown
19) main
20) bringing

Exercise 75a

1) drawing
2) monkeys
3) coast
4) grape
5) turnip
6) port
7) shore
8) depart
9) remain
10) tide

Exercise 75b

11) vine
12) animal
13) donkey
14) wine
15) travel
16) claw
17) return
18) straw
19) monkey
20) field

Crossword No. 73

Letter = A

Crossword No. 74

Letter = N

Crossword No. 75

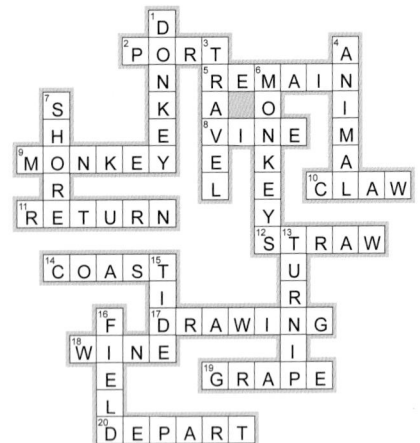

Letter = I

Answers

Key Stage 2 Spelling &
Vocabulary Workbook 4

Exercise 76a
1) prison
2) rather
3) borrow
4) lion
5) crust
6) arrow
7) swan
8) Pardon
9) owl
10) punish

Exercise 76b
11) sorrow
12) enter
13) narrow
14) chicken
15) growl
16) polite
17) forgive
18) path
19) gather
20) rude

Exercise 77a
1) wade
2) hungry
3) carpet
4) snake
5) shallow
6) pillow
7) shake
8) yellow
9) splash
10) pale

Exercise 77b
11) Moss
12) understand
13) stream
14) danger
15) sash
16) trade
17) hunger
18) understood
19) drank
20) anger

Exercise 78a
1) candle
2) April
3) stable
4) marble
5) charge
6) May
7) sport
8) Something
9) handle
10) trust

Exercise 78b
11) stranger
12) form
13) sort
14) someone
15) thorn
16) March
17) large
18) strange
19) sometimes
20) tumble

Crossword No. 76

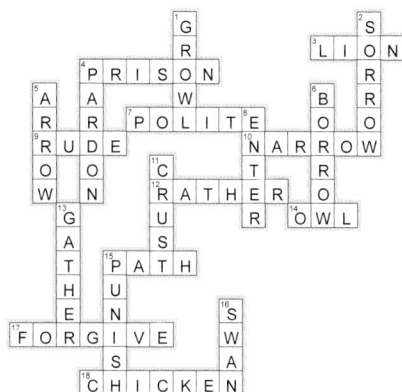

Letter = L

Crossword No. 77

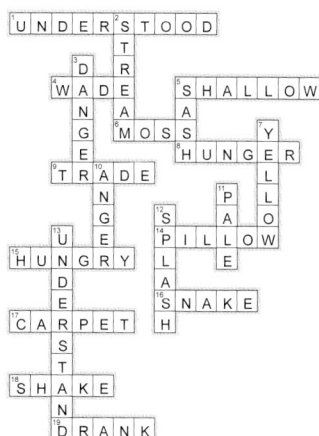

Letter = R

Crossword No. 78

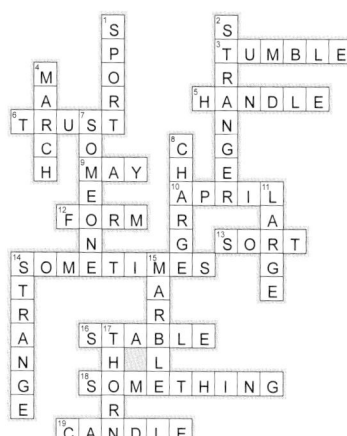

Letter = A

In the Bedroom

1. SLIPPERS	2. MIRROR	3. HANGER	4. DOLLS' HOUSE	5. MOBILE
6. RUG	7. WARDROBE	8. ALARM CLOCK	9. POSTER	10. TOY BOX
11. DRAWER	12. HEADBOARD	13. LAMP	14. PILLOW	15. STOOL

At the Petrol Station

1. WING MIRROR	2. CANOPY	3. CARWASH	4. WINDSCREEN	5. CHARCOAL
6. AERIAL	7. WATERING CAN	8. PETROL PUMP	9. BONNET	10. BUCKET
11. WATER	12. NOZZLE	13. TANKER	14. EXTINGUISHER	15. HOSE

© 2006 Stephen Curran

57

Answers

Exercise 79a

1) unless
2) crumb
3) Thursday
4) busy
5) anybody
6) thumb
7) happen
8) sleepy
9) Sunday
10) lamb

Exercise 79b

11) frosty
12) lucky
13) stormy
14) nobody
15) cloudy
16) comb
17) cannot
18) dusty
19) Friday
20) dirty

Exercise 80a

1) pulled
2) glove
3) brow
4) rolled
5) stove
6) become
7) rolling
8) towel
9) climb
10) steady

Exercise 80b

11) cover
12) power
13) none
14) brain
15) shelter
16) roll
17) cheek
18) shower
19) tower
20) chest

Exercise 81a

1) November
2) ditch
3) everyone
4) July
5) Catch
6) patch
7) learned
8) reached
9) fetch
10) September

Exercise 81b

11) cottage
12) picked
13) match
14) June
15) pudding
16) watch
17) snatch
18) heart
19) picking
20) act

Crossword No. 79

Crossword No. 80

Crossword No. 81

Letter = N

Letter = D

Letter = C

Answers

Key Stage 2 Spelling &
Vocabulary Workbook 4

Exercise 82a
1) blade
2) dull
3) fur
4) care
5) cradle
6) darling
7) careless
8) tender
9) purse
10) useful

Exercise 82b
11) hammer
12) infant
13) gentle
14) bench
15) weak
16) beak
17) useless
18) wire
19) young
20) nurse

Exercise 83a
1) stole
2) stool
3) beef
4) Lunch
5) changed
6) geese
7) eaten
8) broke
9) too
10) cloth

Exercise 83b
11) cheese
12) goose
13) change
14) broken
15) taken
16) blood
17) fool
18) tool
19) buy
20) break

Exercise 84a
1) wristwatch
2) heifer
3) mortar
4) goggles
5) wrapper
6) sledge
7) wren
8) rein
9) handrail
10) springboard

Exercise 84b
11) neighbourhood
12) wrath
13) neigh
14) hedgehog
15) panel
16) wreckage
17) wrestling
18) weird
19) fudge
20) writhe

Crossword No. 82

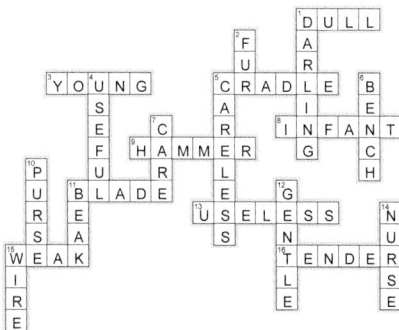

Letter = G

Crossword No. 83

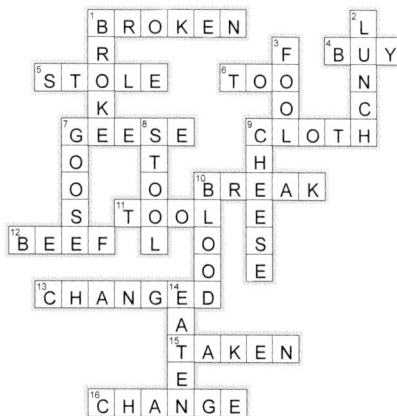

Letter = N

Crossword No. 84

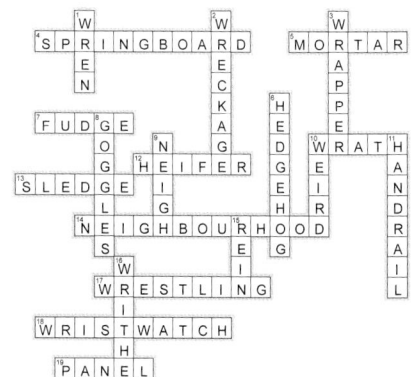

Letter = I

In the Kitchen

1. KETTLE	2. FRIDGE	3. TEAPOT	4. SOCKET	5. BLIND
6. TOASTER	7. BREAD BIN	8. TILES	9. TAPS	10. TEA TOWEL
11. LADLE	12. MUG TREE	13. COOKER	14. CEREAL	15. SAUCEPAN

At the Railway Station

1. COMMUTER	2. SLEEPER	3. FOOTBRIDGE	4. RAIL	5. PORTER
6. PLATFORM	7. BARROW	8. CARRIAGE	9. BILLBOARD	10. SIGNAL
11. BENCH	12. BARRIER	13. KIOSK	14. SIGNBOARD	15. GUARD

© 2006 Stephen Curran

Answers

Exercise 85a
1) gutter
2) gaudy
3) saucepan
4) disobeyed
5) balcony
6) saunter
7) autograph
8) vault
9) barley
10) butterfly

Exercise 85b
11) typist
12) mauve
13) draught
14) sauce
15) flippers
16) spectators
17) sausages
18) spinney
19) parsley
20) haul

Exercise 86a
1) magnifying
2) loiter
3) dictionary
4) ointment
5) terrifying
6) yolk
7) syrup
8) rhythm
9) ration
10) poisonous

Exercise 86b
11) oilfield
12) Boiling
13) rhyme
14) correction
15) joint
16) hidden
17) dyeing
18) hyphen
19) coiled
20) folk

Exercise 87a
1) borough
2) query
3) passport
4) Poppies
5) nodding
6) countries
7) armies
8) gypsies
9) phantom
10) turban

Exercise 87b
11) grabbed
12) worries
13) families
14) turquoise
15) quill
16) quoit
17) pheasant
18) assembly
19) quantity
20) murmur

Crossword No. 85

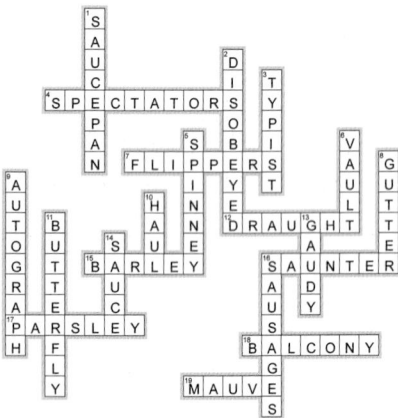

Letter = P

Crossword No. 86

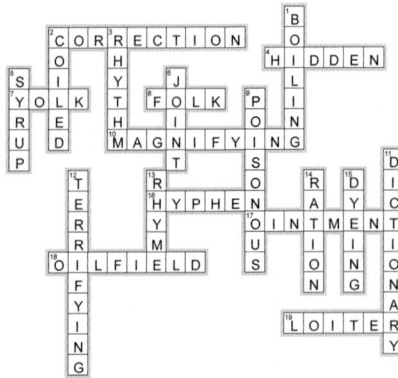

Letter = I

Crossword No. 87

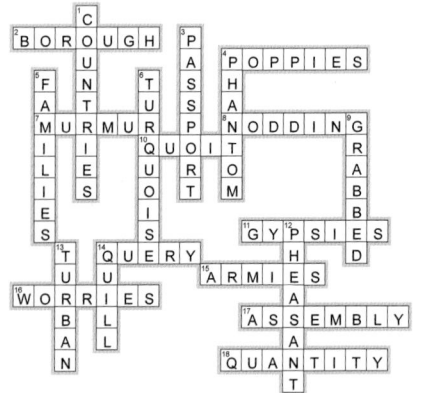

Letter = T

Answers

Exercise 88a

1) deafening
2) buffalo
3) stealthily
4) chaffinch
5) kangaroo
6) porcupine
7) jealousy
8) chauffeur
9) tutor
10) sculptor

Exercise 88b

11) chimpanzee
12) giraffe
13) inventor
14) threatened
15) exaggerate
16) seniors
17) feathers
18) shuffle
19) weasel
20) rhinoceros

Exercise 89a

1) scald
2) surplice
3) blastoff
4) almond
5) kipper
6) survivor
7) skateboard
8) mallet
9) handsaw
10) screwdriver

Exercise 89b

11) surgeon
12) surveyor
13) helmet
14) rhododendron
15) surrounded
16) astronaut
17) drag
18) flamingo
19) surgery
20) surname

Exercise 90a

1) shampoo
2) bleep
3) tent
4) clump
5) quake
6) blackbird
7) blizzard
8) mattress
9) Diesel
10) plug

Exercise 90b

11) nozzle
12) blend
13) quizzes
14) Jazz
15) giggle
16) scone
17) butcher
18) plank
19) lounge
20) dice

Crossword No. 88

Letter = A

Crossword No. 89

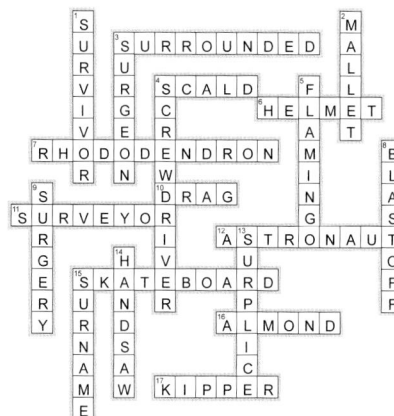

Letter = O

Crossword No. 90

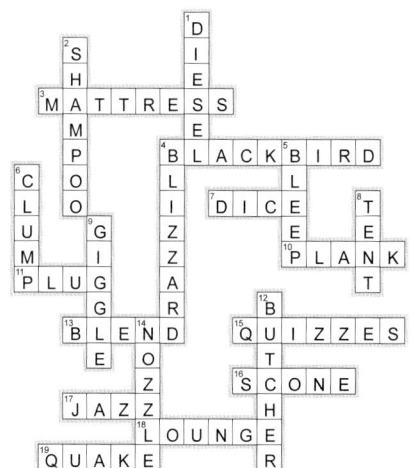

Letter = C

Exercise 91a

1) necklace
2) Wring
3) twinge
4) walks
5) ripped
6) panda
7) mammal
8) drip
9) buzz
10) sheaves

Exercise 91b

11) sharper
12) cruised
13) buzzard
14) brawl
15) sculpture
16) scruffy
17) squat
18) scroll
19) suited
20) walkers

Exercise 92a

1) overstretched
2) notch
3) harder
4) windowsill
5) coldest
6) quarantine
7) faster
8) seaside
9) lighter
10) fluent

Exercise 92b

11) gnaw
12) punctuation
13) wallpaper
14) waterproof
15) drawl
16) higher
17) meadow
18) womb
19) everybody
20) softer

Crossword No. 91

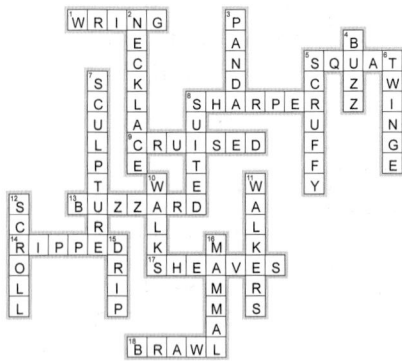

Crossword No. 92

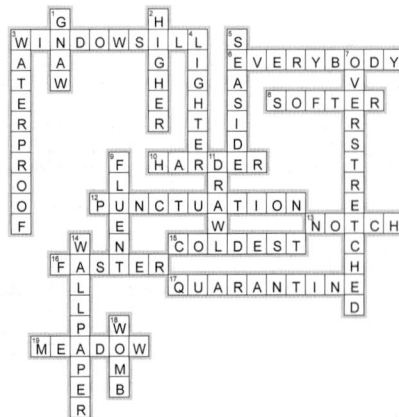

Letter = I

Letter = N

Mystery Word

T C E A N I L R

C L A R I N E T

Mystery Word

A N D C G N I

D A N C I N G

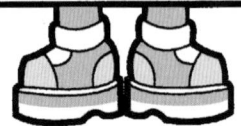

Mystery Word

P I T A O C I N

O P T I C I A N

PROGRESS CHARTS

Scores

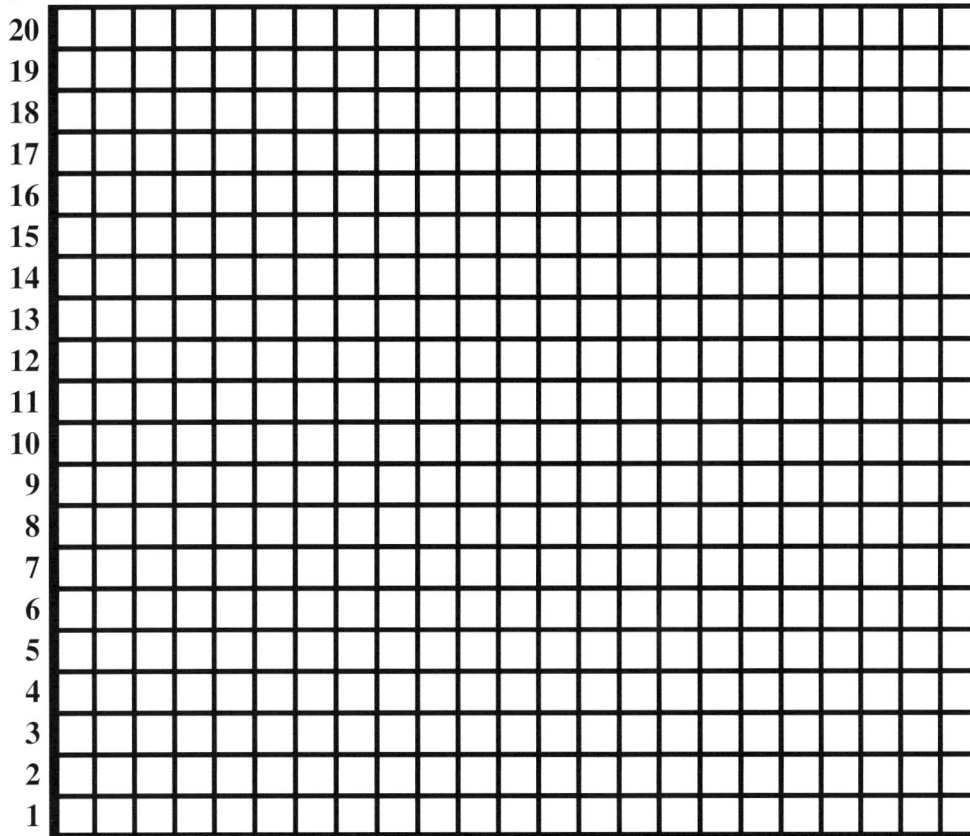

70 71 72 73 74 75 76 77 78 79 80 81 82 83 84 85 86 87 88 89 90 91 92

Exercises

Shade in your score for each exercise on the graph. Add them up for your total score out of 460. Ask an adult to work out the percentage.

Total Score

Percentage

% **A**

Scores

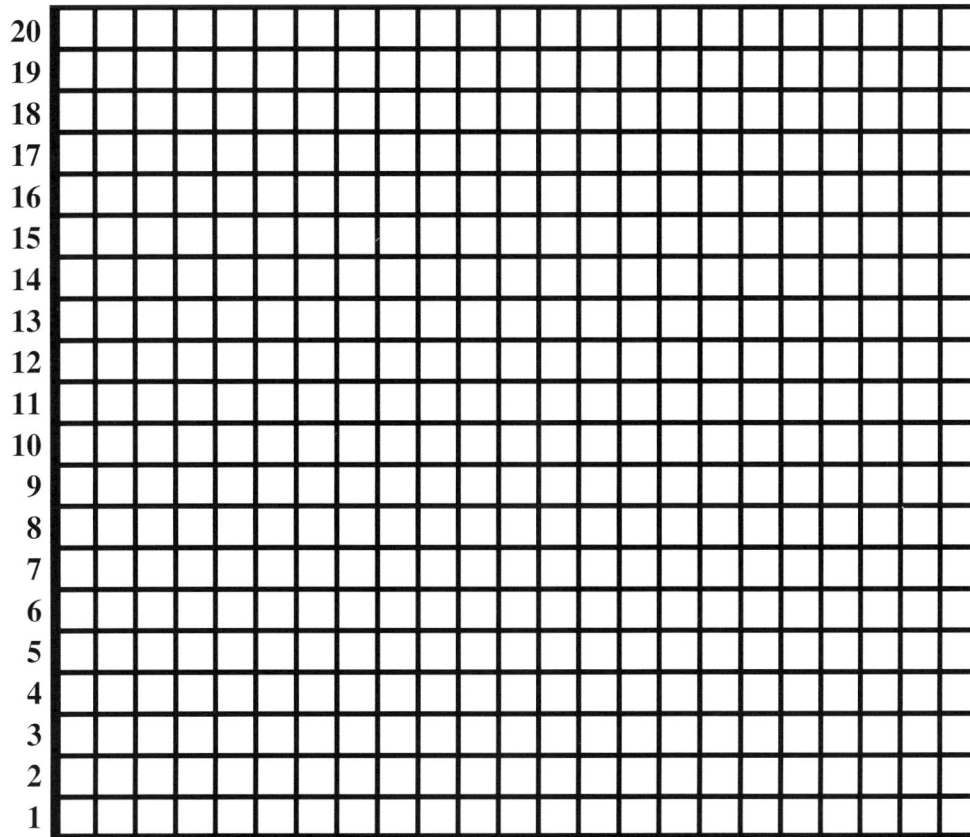

70 71 72 73 74 75 76 77 78 79 80 81 82 83 84 85 86 87 88 89 90 91 92

Crosswords

Shade in your score for each crossword on the graph. Add them up for your total score out of 460.

Total Score

Percentage

% **B**

For the average percentage add %A and %B and divide by 2

Overall Percentage

%

CERTIFICATE OF

ACHIEVEMENT

This certifies

_____

has successfully completed

Key Stage 2
Spelling & Vocabulary

WORKBOOK **4**

Overall percentage
score achieved

[   ] **%**

Comment _____

_____

Signed _____

(teacher/parent/guardian)

Date _____